PRIVATE WORLDS

A REVISED ATLAS

Scott E. Green

SPEAKING VOLUMES, LLS

NAPLES, FLORIDA

2011

PRIVATE WORLDS

ISBN 978-1-61232-040-3

Introduction

This is an expanded edition on my original collection PRIVATE WORLDS.

It includes the original poems plus additional pieces. For those unfamiliar with this book it's a collection of very short poems, usually haikus, that are commentaries on the body of work of various science fiction, fantasy, and horror writers. This expanded edition includes actors, film makers, artists, and other professionals who have worked singularly or collectively in the science fiction-fantasy-horror and related genres. Also most of these new poems are still going to be very short but not necessarily haikus.

ADDAMS' WORLD

Gomez picnicking with the family
at midnight
in a junk yard cemetery
where long dead Desotos'
and Henry J's are buried.

GERRY AND SYLVIA ANDERSON'S WORLD

They are puppet masters
of a universe of heroes…
Brave souls with bodies of wood.
There eyebrow are always raised.

POUL ANDERSON'S WORLD

Warriors of modest nature
striving towards virtue:
Their virtue a mighty tool,
the strength to triumph.

ANTHONY'S WORLD

The multiple faces of God sharing as one
the pattern,
a common universality
waiting to be discovered.

ASMOV'S WORLD

Man moving towards self-perfection.
A perfection set in laughter.
The reflection of perfection
ensconced in gentle shells of steel.
Life is laughter,
even metal can sing out laughter.

A. AUSTIN'S WORLD

An infinite moment
of a gentle world,
far from creatures of cold iron
far from priests of jealous faiths.

BARK'S WORLD

Foibles of man
hidden within the
feathers of the duck.

BAUM'S WORLD

Snares lie by the side
of the road to home.
Waiting for the unwary.

BEAR'S WORLD

Each universe is defined by its cinema.
The silver screen changes but it still exposed
the human condition.

BESTER'S WORLD

The city wraps the pattern
shakes the structure
like a terrier shakes
a rat.
People lie lost in the city
caught in the unfamiliar mazes.
Light of stars
illuminating new streets
streets leading upward
to the waiting sky.

BLISH'S WORLD

The Human Entity
will be a city of infinite
boulevards for fashionable
folk
to promenade under streetlights
of blue-white suns.

BLOCH'S WORLD

Shadows along the sidewalk,
deeper paths hidden
within city streets.

A lonely cry of fear
echoes off buildings.

BOUCHER'S WORLD

Under the light of atomic street lamps
that devour shadows.
There are still hidden pools of darkness
for mystery.

BOVA'S WORLD

Light of star
melts passports.

Black of space
drain the color of skin.

BRACKETT'S WORLD

The true champion
never lacks for enemies,
struggle fatiguing not the soul,
only quickening
desire for greater honor,
the honor that is greater service.

BRYANT'S WORLD

Ocean slashing teeth
drags men into pain
through pain into the future.

BUTLER'S WORLD

Color of skin,
Form of flesh:
barriers stilled over time.

BURROUGH'S WORLD

Mars
is still the world
of adventure
and Africa
is still the home
of its lord.

JOHN CARRADINE'S WORLD

Even the worst monster
and blood thirsty mad scientist
can always remain
the perfect Boston gentlemen.

CHALKER'S WORLD

There will always be
those who call themselves
fools.
Who will do all for what
is right
and claim it is done
but for a six-pack
of Miller Lite.

RAYMOND CHANDLER'S WORLD

The Santa Ana Wind
is a hot wind full of hate.
It leaves murder in its wake.

CHERRYH'S WORLD

Under the rainbow lights
of extravagant galactic metropolises,
there will always be one
to keep polished,
the name of the family
to struggle for
the honor of the family.

CLARKE'S WORLD

The artifact
become the universe.
There are still journeys beyond
and within the
boundaries of the artifact.

CORMAN'S WORLD

Little universe created in a small study
squeeze a few more universe
out of the same set
creating worlds on a frugal budget.

CREASY'S WORLD

Crime haunts the world,
crime haunts London
but the Yard stands firm.

DEL REY'S WORLD

Earth bound
faith bound
humanity away
from the
new lands
that wait for the folk
all around the folk.

DICK'S WORLD

The city full of tears
an ocean of tears.
Time are isles of hope
barely holding their own against
the waves.
Slowly the isles
grow absorbing tears in slow, ever slow
ways.

DISNEY'S WORLD

Boy hood dreams
born under the Midwest sun.
The colors form on the movie screen
and walks among us under Florida sun.

DITKO'S WORLD

The hero
is still of human flesh
still prey to the flesh
still remains a hero.

DOYLE'S WORLD

The hero
is bored
and patiently waiting
for the next challenge.

DUNSANY'S WORLD 1

Eleven horns
tinkle peculiar tones
along motorways.

A magical steed
could be bottle-green Bentleys on Pirellis
instead of pie-bald unicorns
with silvered hooves.

DUNSANY'S WORLD 2

Folk of good will
neither be chaste
or of human flesh
nor pop a pill.

ELGIN'S WORLD

The trickster acts
through the mensch,
her sly wit moves the world
to a better way.

ELLISON'S WORLD

The city is the land of pain.
Most roads lead to it.
Few roads pass it by.

EISNER'S WORLD

On the mean streets of comic book universe
he shows us the human heart
of urban ghetto,
pavement cannot block the strength of soul.

FARMER'S WORLD

The hero is hidden,
among the many
of us.

Grey eyes seeking the
light
not fearing the blinding
flash of self knowledge.

JOHN FORD'S WORLD

Monument Valley
describes
his physical world.
Justice and vengeance
describes
the moral world.

FORT'S WORLD

Ocean depths are the veils
covering
the hidden world, the hidden
truths.

FOX'S WORLD

Right is might
with a blaster,
sword
or fist of steel;
the hero always ends the tale
with the girl (though not if her initials are LL)
and a blaze of Technicolor light.

FREAS' WORLD

Space pirates coming on board with
calculators clench between their
teeth.
Where robots cry over there dead
Creators.

THE CAST OF GHOST HUNTERS' WORLD

Something is strange.
On the cable
Who are you going to call?
ROTO-ROOTER™!!!
And away goes unquiet spirits
down the drain
ROTO-ROOTER.™

GOULART'S WORLD

A wise cracking robot dick
tooling in a Triumph
making warp 5
down I-95.

HAGGARD'S WORLD

The heart of Africa
is the heart of the world.
The womb where heroes
recreate themselves.

HANNA-BARBERA'S WORLD

In their world
talking animals are smarter
than the average human
and wiser in their folly.

HEINLEIN'S WORLD

Bend the Universe
to the will of the one.

Play the one's anthem
the anthem of one.

The one bends the
universe like a cage
around the ego.
Seeing too late the trap.

HERBERT'S WORLD

Thunder of potential
destinies
rolling across the
desert.

HOWARD'S WORLD

Subtle magic
cannot triumph
over the boldness
of strong heroes.

KARLOFF'S WORLD

He moves every slowly.
And speaks in low murmur.
In his world the horror
is always waiting
to explode.

KIRBY'S WORLD

It's a place where heroes are clearly defined
by the bright color of their spandex uniforms.
The villain are defined by their awful grammar.

LANIER'S WORLD

The World's form has
been measured to the
four quarters.

And yet there are still
tall tales of Sumatran rats
and out of work daemons
that still find parts of the world
to be suitable
for hidden quarters.

LAUMER'S WORLD

The universe, like an oyster
lies at man's feet,
his wit the only fork
needed
to gobble its flesh.

BRUCE LEE'S WORLD

In the hands of a master,
craft is shaped to art
vengeance is shaped into justice.

STAN LEE'S WORLD

He is the emperor of universes
so vast
they even make New York City seem small
but never the goodness of its heroes
or the evil
of its villains.

Le GUIN'S WORLD

Universe is a forest,
each path full of danger where treasure is sought,
each path full of treasure where danger is sought.

LEINSTER'S WORLD

One good man
and one good
woman
can still shake
the future for good with a wrench
in the back pocket,
a joke on the lips,
and courage in
the heart.

LEIBER'S WORLD

In a million cities,
under ten thousand suns,
there will always
be an alley
where a billion hands
tentacles, paws,
pseudo-pods
roll the bones,
lay down the odds,
looking for the big,
killing.

LONG'S WORLD

Moon filled night
howls of hounds
above the sky.

LOVECRAFT'S WORLD

A cold wind moves
between suns.

Leviathans playing obscure games
using humanity
in hidden moves.

LYMINGTON'S WORLD

In every count of England
there lives
A dozen INDESCRIBABLE MENACES
OF HUMAN HORROR
chatting amiably with Anglican vicars
about disarmament, the wrongness
of English weather, and
unrestricted immigration.

MACHEN'S WORLD

Ancient hills
hard as flint.
And so are the fey folk
who live there.
Hidden from time.
Hidden from the eyes of others.

ED MCBAIN'S WORLD

Procedure brings order
to the city,
The rules stand between
crime and society.

MEREDITH'S WORLD

Many shadows
of one world,
self-contained in weakness and strength,
unending battles of infinite paths.

MORRISSEY'S WORLD

The artists speaks of
the future
couched in the tales of
the past.

NORTON'S WORLD 1

A laconic tabby with opal eyes
finds bits of magic
to toy with
in obscure corners
of Merlin's motor home.

NORTON'S WORLD 2

Broken stone circles
still dream of power.

NORTON'S WORLD 3

Slums don't bar
the progress
of heroes.

PHILLIP NOWLAND'S WORLD

The guest for adventure
always has to wait
for next week.

PANGBORN'S WORLD

Forests covers man's work
like a grasshopper leaping from
the grass.
Civilization worms its way back
through the groves of oak
and through caribou herds
The fox's bark drowned out
again by men.

POE'S WORLD

The streets of desolate
are haunted
by the caw of
ravens hearts.
Whisper of ghost love
fog these eyes.

E.H. PRICE'S WORLD

The future
will be one of lacquered
spaceships
and cities powered by
the breath
of indulgent Dragons.

Scott E. Green

VINCENT PRICE'S WORLD

His villains
hide their sorrow
in their hearts.

PRIEST'S WORLD

Time is like a weight
crushing bones,
cracking souls,
residue finding its
way into the future.

REYNOLD'S WORLD

Humanity builds its
own prison,
The wonders
at the bars
before its eyes.

ROBERTS' WORLD

The minuet
starts,
the partners
move on the
dance floor.
in a pirouette
man is flung
out to the stars,
in the next
man is flung
back.
The dance
continues,
the dancers continue indefinitely.

ROHMER'S WORLD

In Limehouse shadows
he waits
until he once again
walks the streets
of Shanghai.

RUSS' WORLD

Humanity shall make the
universe a home,
but who shares the home
while away?

SABATINI'S WORLD

A world where justice is found
on a point of a sword.
A world where romance is found
in the rustle of crinoline.
A world where bravery counts.

SIEGEL- SCHUSTER'S WORLD

Out of the death of a world
is born.
The champion of another world
yet with the strength to bend
steel
he can never show his love.

SERLING'S WORLD

The world where hatefulness is danger,
where love is survival.
Yet there are those who embrace hate,
biding their time until the universe crushed them
or the embrace love to save themselves.
sometimes, it's never too late.

SILVERBERG'S WORLD

The frontier is inward,
each human is an infinite universe,
each with unnumbered lands to explore.
The city brings together the universes
The city is the sum of creation.

SIMAK'S WORLD

Our past lies in the
forest
moving among the
fields.
Our futures includes
the forest, preserve
the fields.

SLADEK'S WORLD

Eyes followed him
across the room
on tiny, padded feet.

CORDWAINER SMITH'S WORLD

On the back of beasts
man continues onward.

THORNE SMITH'S WORLD

Sophisticated Spirits
sipping ghostly goblets
of dead mobsters' bootleg spirits
and laughing at the feeble morals
of flesh-bound mortals.

STROKER'S WORLD

Night muffles the screams,
a hunter seeking blood
pride turned to
unending hunger.

TOHO STUDIO'S WORLD

Men in giant rubber monster suits
crushing Tokyo again and again.
Sometimes
they're the heroes.
Sometimes
they are the villains.

STURGEON'S WORLD

The hero knows
90% of everything is junk.
I does not stop the hero from
seeking the 10%.

VANCE'S WORLD 1

Edifice of words,
carefully selected,
propelling man into
the future.

VANCE'S WORLD 2

A robot
sipping motor oil
from a bone china cup.

WATSON'S WORLD

The soul pierces the boundary
leaving the flesh behind.

KARL EDWARD WAGNER

The whole world
points to him.
Cain
for his crime
imprisoned in his immortality.

RICHARD WAGNER'S WORLD

Fire of hate
Frozen
In ice.

M.W. WELLMAN'S WORLD

Music poured from silver strings
and a true heart.
The only barrier against
the old gods who haunt
wooded hills and the song
of the lark.

Scott E. Green

WELL'S WORLD

The man is triumphant,
The state elevates the
race high
like a titanic elephant.

The height is dizzying,
man falls beneath
the elephant's feet,
only the jumbled ruins
are left,
like those of ancient Ceylon.

JAMES WHITE'S WORLD

Intelligence
is nothing
if it cannot
heal.

T.H. WHITE'S WORLD

The matter of Britain is
the matter of the world
the matter of love.

WILHELM'S WORLD

A woman is a bird of fire
illuminating the world
a phoenix not consumed
in self-destruction
dedicated to creation.

WILLIAMSON'S WORLD

The toaster on the kitchen
table
is a deadlier foe
than the wolf
scratching at the door.

ZELAZNY'S WORLD

Face of man
Mask of god
the Mask liberated
the Mask binds tears
To the Face.

About the Author

Scott E. Green has been active as a poet in the science fiction/fantasy/horror genres for over thirty five years. He is the author of the only reference book on science fiction/fantasy/horror poetry, CONTEMPORARY SCIENCE FICTION, FANTASY, AND HORROR POETRY; A RESOURCE GUIDE AND BIOGRAPHICAL DIRECTORY(Westport, CT; 1989,Greenwood). In addition he has done entries on poetry for other reference books.

Green is a past President of the Science Fiction Poetry Association. Over the years he has chaired many panels on poetry at science fiction conventions including several World Science Fiction Conventions, World Fantasy Conventions, and World Horror Conventions. He has also done many readings including at the Library of Congress, Boston Public Library and Nashua (NH) Public Library.

www.ingramcontent.com/pod-product-compliance
Lightning Source LLC
LaVergne TN
LVHW091211080426
835509LV00006B/943